# Bulletin Board Ideas

Bonne Morris

**Bulletin Board Ideas**
Copyright © 1991 by Abingdon Press

**ISBN 0-687-04553-3**

Design, layout, and illustrations by John Boegel

MANUFACTURED IN THE UNITED STATES OF AMERICA

# CONTENTS

## ACKNOWLEDGMENT

A special word of thanks goes to both the staff and the members of Forest Lake United Methodist Church in Tuscaloosa, Alabama. Their kind words of approval have always doubly repaid me for my efforts.

As you embark upon this loving gesture for your church, thank God that you were chosen for this unique mission! May this sourcebook offer both inspiration and insight for your church bulletin boards. ■

# THE NEED FOR CHURCH BULLETIN BOARDS

The power of God's Spirit will overcome anyone inside an attractive church. Surrounded by that presence, one is apt to feel a sense of peace and contentment.

An attractive bulletin board will help to issue an invitation of welcome to any visitor. The physical church home suggests the type of congregation. If the church's appearance fails to extend a welcome, what might a visitor expect to receive from its members?

The church bulletin board has another, more practical use.

Church members have not only a need, but also a right to be informed about their church's activities. This is imperative, if they are to identify with their church home.

Wedding and birth announcements, obituaries, and awards should be posted. Notices, memos, and correspondence also should be available to the members.

## THE CENTRAL BOARD

Every church should have a bulletin board in a central location. Usually found in the dining hall or entry, this board will be a handy reference for all church members.

Each month, change the paper color and title the board with the new month's name. Keep your church informed with these items of interest:

● **A Monthly Calendar of Church Activities.** Be alert to revisions, and note such changes neatly.

● **Photos of New Members.** On a small piece of paper posted neatly below the photos, list the names, addresses, and phone numbers.

● **Notices.** Keep these items current, and return out-of-date material for office filing or discarding.

● **Newspaper Articles/Photos.**
Clip these daily and post them once or twice a week.
Underline name(s) with pen or marker. In a journal or notebook, record:
*Name of person(s).*
*Date.*
*Title of article or a sentence summary.*
*Family member name(s) for future reference—spouse of person, parent(s) of child.*

● **Personal Photos.** Handle all photos carefully and return them promptly to the owner, or designate a spot in the office for their convenient pick-up.

Attach photos carefully to the board, using tacks directly above and below the photo edge; do not mar the picture.

## THE CLASSROOM BOARD

Bulletin boards add pride and spirit to any classroom! They also serve as an excellent resource tool for teachers:

Open a new study topic with appropriate maps, charts, and pictures. This will assist in later recall of the material.

Also use bulletin boards to motivate members to ask questions and share ideas during group discussions.

Let the young learners proudly display prized drawings. Both classrooms and students are transformed!

# THREE STEPS TOWARD A NEW BULLETIN BOARD

**The job is easy,
if you follow these steps!**

# 1.

**D**etermine the amount of background paper needed. Measure the board's dimensions and add a margin edge of 1 to 2 inches. Note the size for future reference and cut the needed amount.

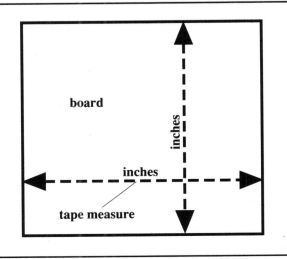

# 2.

**A**void wrinkled paper. Roll up the piece loosely. Now align the margin next to the board edge and secure it with tacks. Then slowly unroll the paper, smoothing out ripples with a gentle, sweeping hand. Reinforce the paper with additional tacks. Then staple around the edge and remove the tacks.

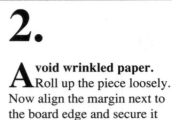

**rolled paper**

**margin**

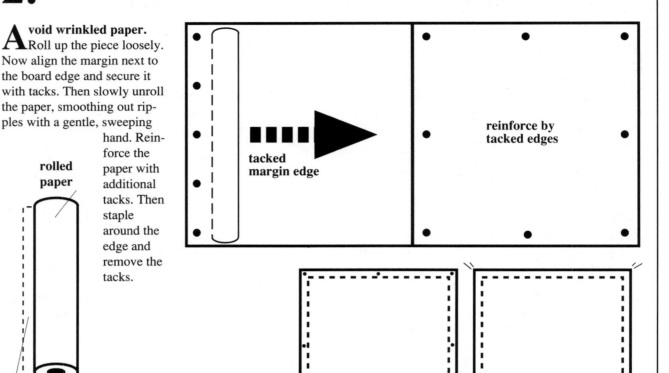

**tacked margin edge**

**reinforce by tacked edges**

# 3.

**T**ack a commercial double border strip directly below the top border edge. You now have your top margin, revealed when you remove the strip. Single border strips against the left and right margins serve as temporary edge definition and helps when spacing lines.

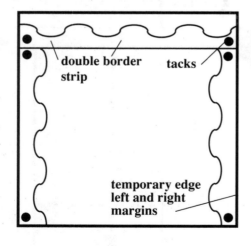

**double border strip**

**tacks**

**temporary edge left and right margins**

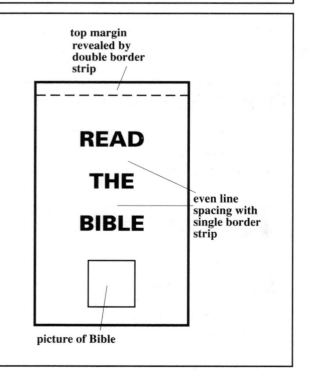

**top margin revealed by double border strip**

**READ**

**THE**

**BIBLE**

**even line spacing with single border strip**

**picture of Bible**

# PREPARATION

## THE TOOLBOX

For maximum efficiency, each volunteer should have a separate "toolbox." A plastic tool caddy or large shoe box is an ideal choice for holding your essentials.

● **Include the following items:**
*scissors*
*tape measure*
*thumb tacks*
*small ruler*
*rubber bands*
*pencil(s)*
*staple remover*
*stapler*
*paper clips*
*fine point pen (black or blue)*
*felt pens (black, blue, red)*
*felt markers (black, blue, red)*
*removable tape*
*tissues*
*small change*

Label the contents to guarantee against a mix-up with church items. This also allows easy identification during group work.

## PAPER ITEMS

**Keep your supplies—border strips, letters, numerals, up to date!**

Making a supply of paper items need not be a time-consuming job! Quiet time usually reserved for television or reading can be spent tracing or cutting.

A small box or tote kept near a favorite chair should contain scissors, construction paper, fine-point pen, and tracing stencils (2" stencils, found in school supply stores).

Commercial border strips, sold in boxes, easily separate for use as a single border pattern, which can be used in tracing.

Later, when needed, those extra letters will be ready for use. A snip or two is all it will take for that much needed letter!

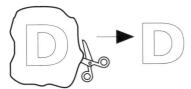

Border strips and alphabet letters can be kept in shoe boxes. Store them separately by color.

Recycle used border strips. Clip tacked or stapled edges at a diagonal angle. Have they faded? Turn them over! Are they worn? Hide them beneath new border strips for contrast.

Keep your alphabet letters housed in separate envelopes. For aid in quick reference, mark the outside envelope in the corresponding letter color. Alphabetize within each color group.

Reuse letters in good condition. They are an invaluable resource. File by letter and mark the envelope with the appropriate letter, preceded by the word Used.

Build up a quick supply of items with the help of church members! Women's or youth groups will gladly assist, when encouraged by a nearby refreshment table! Provide a bounty of scissors, pens and paper. Delegate a helper to file by envelope, so that letters/numerals will be at hand for ready decoration!

## TYPING OR PRINTING

Sometimes lettering is not appropriate for a bulletin board idea. Instead, type or print the message.

Refer to an office handbook when typing.

When printing, try to work in a quiet place at a time when you are not rushed. This will minimize errors.

● **Have the proper supplies nearby:**
*dictionary*
*unlined white paper*
*lined sheet*
*ruler*
*pencil/pen/marker*
*eraser*

Allow for even margins top and bottom, left and right.

Skip lines between sentences, titles, subtitles, and paragraphs.

Be consistent in letter shape, letter size, and spacing between letters, words, and sentences.

## PICTURES

Pictures and patterns are a mainstay of your bulletin boards. Begin now to amass your collection. To prevent loss, house them in clasped manila envelopes.

Newspapers and coloring books are excellent sources for patterns. Colorful pictures of flowers, animals, and more abound in magazines.

Sunday school teaching aids are your most valuable resource when in need of religious subject matter. An elementary study book might offer a picture of the twelve disciples. Highlights of Holy Week would be listed in an adult study series.

Take responsibility for the posters and pictures which sometimes accompany Sunday school literature. If it has not already been done, start now to file and store these for many uses in the years to come!

## THUMBTACKS

Keep these "points" in mind whenever using thumbtacks for board display.

Choose tacks of the same color and use quality tacks. Reserve worn tacks for less obvious use beneath a posted item: Fold the paper edge and place the item for posting. Lift it up to reveal the margin edge (inches will vary); then secure.

Avoid tempting tiny fingers. Resort to either tape or a stapler when working in preschool classrooms.

Rely upon thumb tacks, too, for punctuation marks-an excellent period-or as apples on a tree, buttons on an elevator, and so on!

# READY TO BEGIN?

Place your letters directly next to the bottom edge of the top border strip, to ensure proper alignment. Border strip patterns are a handy guide to letter placement. Count the number of letters in a given line. Then count the number of scallops/indentions of the border strip. Assign each letter to a place (large letters may require more room). Allow for an even margin on each side, as well as between words.

Use a single perforated commercial strip between lines. The tacked ends, when removed, reveal single-line spacing. Lift the strip neatly and place again for each line needed.

Save an unperforated border strip, at least 45 inches long, to be used as a margin guide. Label it as a toolbox item and reinforce the back with masking tape to prevent separation. Replace this strip when it is worn.

Place items at the proper eye level. Special consideration should be given both to older members and to children. Older members, for example, would appreciate boards of their concern on the first floor whenever possible. A child would notice items at a lower eye level.

Upon completion of the board, place the outside border as a final step.

**Emphasize your bulletin board message in several ways.**
*Underline word(s) or sentence(s) with marker highlights or paper strips. Use*
    *Word color*
    *Letter color*

*Size of word, as in "BIG"*
*Position of word(s)*—Look **UP** to Jesus.

Working with large bulletin boards can prove a challenge! Don't let them overwhelm you; instead, consider their versatility!

Use them in their entirety or divide them into smaller sections.

They are invaluable when faced with paper clutter. Almost any leftover pieces in good condition will help to provide an attractive board.

Using a very small strip of paper? Let it offer a simple WELCOME, or perhaps a name from the Bible will stir a mind.

If a piece has an even outside margin edge, let it work for you! Placed as the outer edge of your board, it offers a straight line for easy border placement!

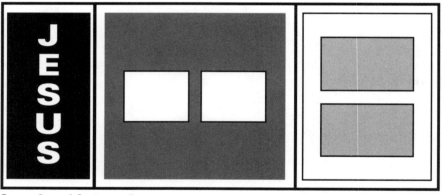

**Large board features three separate boards**

---

## HELPFUL HINTS

Always keep these rules in mind. Your reward will be personal job satisfaction and increased work efficiency.

**1. Establish a regular schedule, approved by the church staff.**

**2. Alert the church office, should you need to change or cancel a work visit.**

**3. Stop by the office when you arrive and when you depart.**

**4. Begin work promptly.** A busy office deserves your co-operation. Remind others of your work location. Should the need arise-a personal phone call, perhaps-you can be found quickly!

**5. Be considerate when working near others!**

**6. Honor church supplies!** Rely on your toolbox. Reuse items, if possible. Cut paper carefully; accuracy will eliminate waste. Notify the church office *before* an item needs replacement and allow ample time for reprints or copies.

# ANIMALS OF THE BIBLE

**N**ot to be overlooked in Bible study are the animals, so important to the way people of those times lived. Include a picture of each animal, as well as a description of how the animal was used or appropriate verse(s) that mention it. Information may be gathered from a number of books. Animals such as the dove, rooster, lion, or sheep would make an attractive board. Add others as space permits.

# "ASK AND IT WILL BE GIVEN TO YOU."

**B**ible verses are an ideal choice for any bulletin board! They are attractive, versatile, educational, and inspirational.

**Display them anytime:**
**Seasonal**-holiday celebrations
**Topical**-appropriate verses
**Personal**-words of comfort, hope.
**Educational**-to help retain study material!

### SCRIPTURE REFERENCES

Apply Bible scripture to any topical bulletin board. Let God's personal word further extend your message.

Appropriate verses are easy to obtain. Consult your pastor or Bible dictionaries and other such books for ready information.

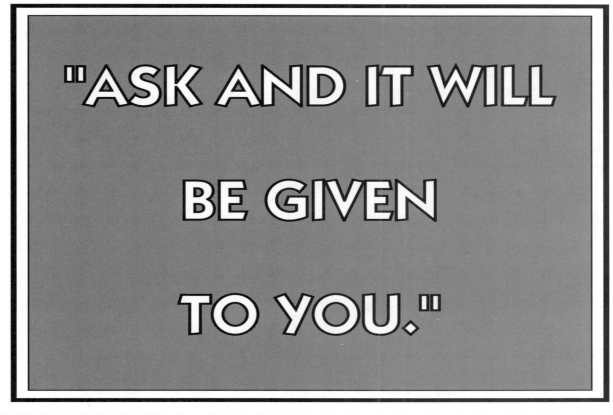

# BRUSH UP ON THE BIBLE

R einforce the idea that Bible reading is important to us. Use a broom, with words for "debris" written neatly on strips of paper.

"Problems" written on the strips of "debris":

*afraid*
*lonely*
*in need of forgiveness*
*doubt*
*anger*

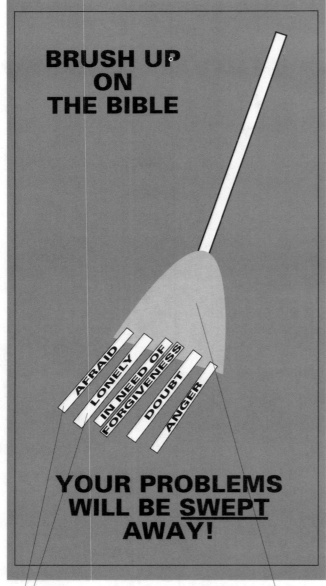

strips for debris—print
problems on them

broom pattern of
colored paper

# GRIN AND SHARE IT!
# READ THE BIBLE

picture of family sharing
the Bible or of the Bible
itself

Encourage daily Bible reading in the homes of church members.

# FRIENDS FROM THE BIBLE

Acquaint children with Bible personalities through an attractive chart with facts about someone from the Bible. Title the chart with the biblical person's name. Illustrate with a picture, if possible.

**FRIENDS FROM THE BIBLE**

THE LIFE OF JESUS

chart

# DOES LIFE NEEDLE YOU? READ THE BIBLE!

The "point" of this message is to motivate everyone to read the Bible! Illustrate with a picture of the Bible. Emphasize the word *needle*!

thread—curled piece of construction paper

needle—gray paper strip

DOES LIFE NEEDLE YOU?

READ THE BIBLE!

picture of the Bible

# BE INVOLVED IN THE BIBLE

Remind church members to make the Bible an active part of their lives

**BE INVOLVED IN THE BIBLE**

**BELIEVE IN THE WORD.**
**LEARN FROM THE WORD.**
**MEDITATE UPON THE WORD.**
**SHARE THE WORD.**

# EARLY WAYS IN EARLY DAYS

**E**nhance young children's understanding of life during Bible times. This board, illustrated with pictures and brief descriptions, will show how people lived long ago. Enlist class help! Let children submit their own drawings, gathered from ideas in group discussion. Post a name/description label strip with each picture. A chart would look nice. Print examples given by the class.

## LET'S LEARN ABOUT . . .

Encourage study and reading of the Bible with chapter profiles. Title with the name of a chapter. Add the following:

1. Picture of event or story from the chapter.
2. Bible verse.
3. Description of chapter.
4. Question to motivate reading!

picture

Bible verse/description/questions
Note: Give version of Bible used.

## READ BETWEEN THE LINES/THE BIBLE ANSWERS

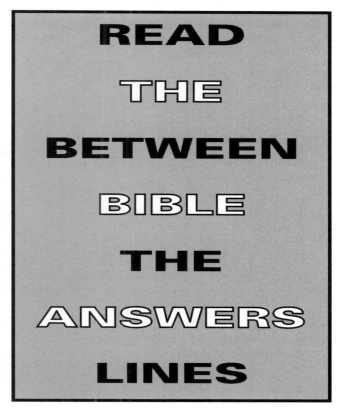

We need to turn to the Bible whenever we have problems. To stress board message, use a different color for each statement (i.e., READ BETWEEN THE LINES—yellow; THE BIBLE ANSWERS—green).

picture of Bible

**MARK YOUR PLACE!**

various color paper "bookmarks"

## MARK YOUR PLACE

We, too, have a place in the Bible; and it, in turn, has a place in our lives. As we practice these statements, we show that we do belong in God's Word!

## PLAY IT SAFE/READ THE BIBLE AT HOME

Use this baseball theme during the summer. Use green paper background with white border and colored letters for contrast. Use square shape for "base." Paper strips accent nicely.

grass-green paper background

white paper baselines

white paper bases

## WHEN YOU MAKE THE BIBLE NUMBER ONE . . .

picture of a Bible

The Bible should always be at the top of any summer reading list. Choose warm colors for display.

# WHEN GOD IS HERE, WE NEED NOT FEAR

blue background paper        balloon        white paper clouds

W ith the Lord in our life, we need not be afraid. Letting go of balloons is an idea to show release, with God's help, from unnecessary fears-sickness, loneliness, etc.

**FEAR examples:**
1. loneliness
2. to be unloved
3. to be afraid
4. sickness

Use blue background paper. Write each "fear" neatly on a plain index card and fasten to the string at the edge of balloon. Decorate with one or two clouds to show sky illusion.

## BE OF GOOD CHEER

With the start of any year, everyone strives to put aside old ways. We will succeed if we treat ourselves and others with love. The following examples provide an excellent check-up method!

BE OF GOOD CHEER

1. VISIT A FRIEND.

2. DEVELOP INTERESTS.

3. HELP OTHERS

4. STUDY THE BIBLE

5. ATTEND WORSHIP.

WHEN YOU BEGIN
THE YEAR!

## FAITH

A hot air balloon is just the right prop for a board on faith. Post it with this message.
**FAITH**
**Take hold of your faith.**
**Don't let go . . .**
**You'll find that you land**
**safely below!**

**Colored paper clouds**

**Balloon of colored
paper strips**

# FENCES

**F**ences are a common sight in any area neighborhood-even in our own lives! This simple prop lends a strong message to this bulletin board. Decorate with appropriately sized fences and description.

### HIGH FENCES (RESTRICTION)
We can't see over it and are blocked from the good life God intended for us.

### LOW PRICES (IRRESPONSIBILITY)
A low fence might cause us to stumble about, with lack of purpose.

### BROKEN FENCE
### (CONFUSION AND TEMPTATION)
A fence full of gaps create chaos and confusion.

### FENCE WITH LOCKED GATE
### (HOPELESSNESS)
We would tend to give up, facing doom, failure, and remorse.

### FENCE WITH OPEN GATE (GROWTH)
This gate allows us to grow, always open to opportunity. It permits us to open to the good in life, but closes out the bad. No matter our height, this fence will match our size!

### DIRECTIONS FOR MAKING FENCES
*Materials needed:*
*ruler,*
*fine/medium point pen,*
*scissors*

*"X" alphabet letter (dark color)*
*two paper strips (sized to fit paper/card)*
*five plain white index cards*
*(no larger than   4 X 6")*

1. **High fence**— one index card
2. **Low fence**— one index card with trimmed margin edge (of 1 to 1 1/2")

3. **Broken fence**— one index card, but with paper strip "flap" to resemble loose board! Place atop "fence"; bend slightly, or "curl" with finger for dimension.
4. **Locked (gate) fence**— place" X" (signifies lock/key) on index card; center slightly to either the right or left of the middle.
5. **Open (gate) fence**— place paper strip on index card, fashioned in the form of a "gate." Bend to show that this fence is open!

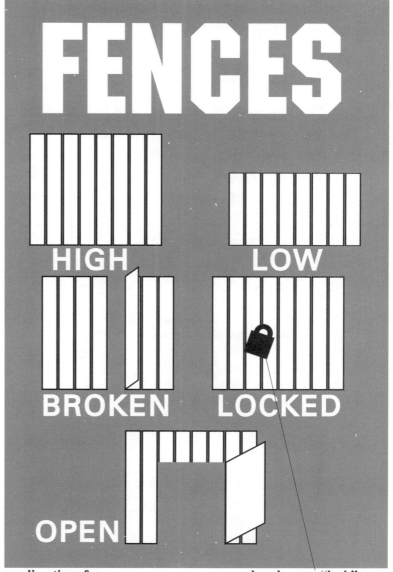

see directions for
index card "fences"

colored paper "lock"

# INTERRUPTIONS

Spell "Interruptions" in different colored letters (according to syllable sound). From this board, we will become aware of the ideas listed.

## INTERRUPTIONS

1. LEARN FROM THEM.
2. REFLECT UPON THEM.
3. PRAY FOR GUIDANCE.
4. ACCEPT THEM.
5. BEGIN  ANEW.

# MY HEART BELONGS TO YOU!

Spread love around your church! Below the title, feature hearts with a Christian message of love. Rely upon Bible verses; no commercialism is allowed. Older children might cite personal examples, telling others what love means to them. As with any assistance from Sunday school classes, allow ample time.

paper hearts                    Christian message/ Bible verse(s)

# PROBLEMS ARE LIKE LOLLIPOPS!

This humorous message will remind members that life's problems can be faced! We need not turn away in despair, for with God's help, problems will dissolve just as lollipops do when we lick them!

colored paper lollipop and stick

# RECOGNIZE YOUR RAINBOW!

**R**ecall and give thanks for the good in our lives. Remembering these good things-like a rainbow-will brighten any day! It should serve as a reminder to give thanks to God.

Use strips of background paper for 7 color bands cut in half-circle shapes. For each smaller size, decrease by 1 inch.

**On each band, print one of the following:**
*home*
*health*
*friends*
*family*
*church*
*personal relation-ship with Jesus*
*job and talents*

# OPEN UP TO A SHUT-IN!

**R**ecognize the shut-in members common to every church. This board will relay the importance of remembering them in our thoughts, prayers, deeds, and visits.

Picture a pretty neighborhood street. Focus on the homes of two dear little older people who are shut-ins.

Cut 2 equal-sized rectangles for the houses and 2 equal-sized triangles for the roofs. Each house should correspond with the other—that is, a dark roof set atop a light house, and vice versa.

Decorate with door and window patterns. Place a picture of each shut-in at a window. Put bushes in front of the houses.

Use white strips of paper for the fences. A sidewalk of gray paper, should lead up to the front doors. Run another sidewalk outside the fences.

Use green and blue for the board's main color scheme, to portray sky and lawn. A chimney of the house color should be atop each roof.

Identify each shut-in with a name written on a cloud.

Adorn one yard with an apple tree. Red thumb tacks are excellent as apples!

An information card can be placed near the side. Names of people to visit or who to contact if interested in visitation can be listed.

print name of shut-in
on each white cloud

green bushes

tree with
red thumbtack apples

## PROBLEMS PILING UP?

**E**veryone has problems! This board would look nice during fall, when our lawns are scattered with leaves! If we can sweep up our problems as we sweep up our leaves, the Lord will gladly receive them. On leaf stencil patterns, you might wish to neatly print examples of problems common to all.

**Problem examples to be printed on leaves:**
*1. being in need*
*2. ill family member*
*3. worry*
*4. feeling greed*
*5. temptation*

## PROBLEMS PILING UP?

## LEAF THEM TO THE LORD!

## RELATIONSHIPS SCORE . . .

This tennis theme might be used in the spring or summer.

## "WEED" OUT THE PROBLEMS IN YOUR LIFE

Use a garden theme, and post around the growing season. Just as there are weeds in yards, so there might be such things in our hearts.

Use strips of paper for the weeds. "Envy, jealousy, hate," etc., can be printed neatly on the strips.

cut out strips of paper for "weeds."

## ALL FOR FUN AND FUN FOR ALL!

Our Lord recognizes the importance of fun and happy times, which promote fellowship among church members. Use the following idea to remind everyone of up-coming events. Details of the events can be spelled out or printed neatly on a chart attached to the bulletin board.

# A HEAD ABOVE THE BEST

Want a novel way to welcome a new staff member? Introduce him or her to your congregation with this clever board! Place a recent photo and brief details on a sheet of paper. Tape message next to this. Fashion as a billboard by placing 2 or 3 inch-wide strips of paper as an outdoor pole. Adapt pole length to fit the board and center in the middle. Add houses and buildings to resemble a street. Adorn with sidewalk and road. Place car on road, making sure to add black streaks for exhaust! Tack the note below.

**NOTE:** Let's offer our blessings to (*name*) as (*he/she*) starts down the road as (*job title*).

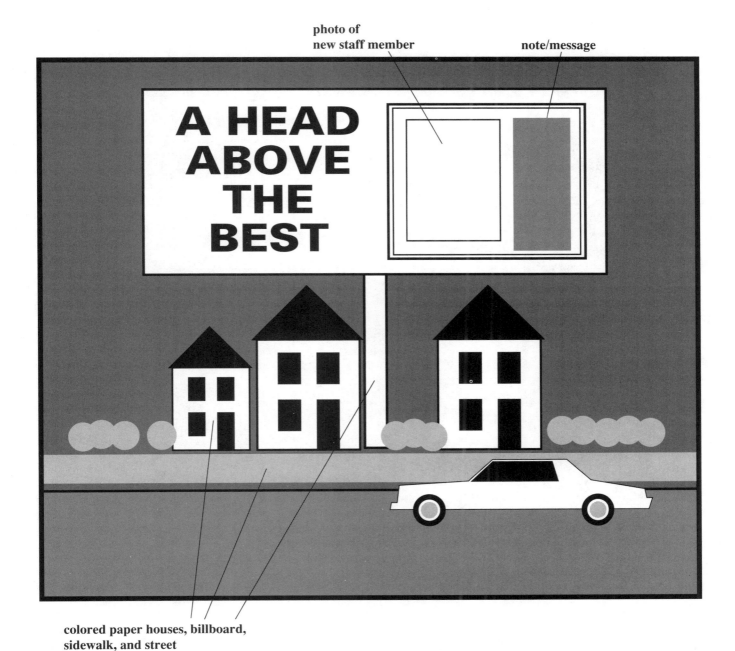

photo of
new staff member

note/message

A HEAD
ABOVE
THE
BEST

colored paper houses, billboard,
sidewalk, and street

## WELCOME, VISITOR!

# WELCOME, VISITOR!

PERHAPS A FRIENDLY FACE,

ISN'T IN ITS PLACE

TO LOVINGLY WELCOME YOU.

WE HURRY ABOUT,

RUSHING IN AND OUT,

YET WE WANT TO SPEAK TO YOU!

SO LET'S USE THIS WALL,

DECKED IN ITS COLORFUL HUES,

TO SPEAK FOR US ALL.

AS CHURCH MEMBERS,

MANNERS WE REMEMBER!

**OUR WELCOME AND HELLO TO YOU!**

## AT THE BAT IS WHERE IT'S AT!

**I**nterest church members in the summer baseball team. Use green paper for the board; white for the letters, shapes, and border strips.

green background paper

playing field and
illustration                    information

## ODDS AND ENDS

**I**n some church buildings, a separate room may be devoted to the craft materials so often relied upon during class projects. Use the following idea to promote use of these items!

(Name) refers to designated name of the room—i.e., supply room, resource room. "Odds and ends" remind members of the many items at their disposal.

illustrate with cut-out pictures
of odds and ends

# WELCOME TO . . .

**pamphlets, photos, information**

**P**romote your church home. Feature information about what the church offers as it welcomes both members and visitors. A background of church history, as well as pamphlets, brochures, and photos could be included.

## MY CHURCH HOME

**T**o a very young child, a church can be overwhelming. Now is the time to help children learn about God's house. It has so much to offer!

Feeling happy at church is vital to the foundation of good Christian education. Start now by letting children post drawings of the ways they feel happy inside God's home! Include a sentence description; label with child's name.

**childrens' drawings with label description**

# HOLIDAY MEMORIES

Strengthen children's roots in their church home by displaying their artistic ability. Ask the children to draw a favorite holiday memory. All should feature the same holiday, and all art paper used should be of the same quality. Emphasize that no commercialism is allowed.

**A group discussion beforehand might arouse appropriate ideas. Some to be considered:**
*Sharing a holiday with a brand-new baby family member.*
*Enjoying a talk with a grandparent while opening gifts.*
*Singing favorite songs and carols with family.*
*Listening to an adult read from the Bible about the birth of Baby Jesus.*
*Making Christmas gifts for a loved one.*
*Watching holiday food being prepared—and of the moment they helped!*
*Taking a basket of food to an older friend.*
*Travels to a loved one for holiday celebration.*
Other thoughts may come to their minds as these ideas are tossed forth. Frame each picture with construction paper and add label.

child's drawing with
label description

# LET US GIVE THANKS

horn of plenty made of
various color paper ovals

drawings or cut-out pictures
of food items

Remember Thanksgiving with this colorful board idea. To thank God for our bounty, make a horn of plenty, adding plenty of fruits and vegetables!
Patterns for food items can be traced from coloring books and copied from grocery-store ads. A horn of plenty can be made from construction paper. Size will be determined by board space.

# HE IS NOT HERE
# BUT HE IS RISEN

Celebrate Easter and Christ's victory from the cross! Accent cross with white paper lily. Place message on either side.

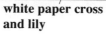
white paper cross
and lily

*For bulletin boards with an Easter theme, you can construct your own Easter lilies. Refer to the diagram on this page and the patterns on page 29.*

### CONSTRUCTION

1. Trace patterns and enlarge if necessary.
2. Cut out patterns.
3. Cut a 12" yellow pipe cleaner into thirds. These will be the stamens.
4. Twist the green pipe cleaner around the three yellow pipe cleaners (stamens).
5. Fold the bottom part of the lily around the stamens and the green pipe-cleaner stem, then staple.
6. Curl lily petals with a pencil.
7. Staple two leaves to the pipe-cleaner stem.

### MATERIALS

construction paper

12" green pipe cleaners

12" yellow pipe cleaners

stapler

scissors

glue

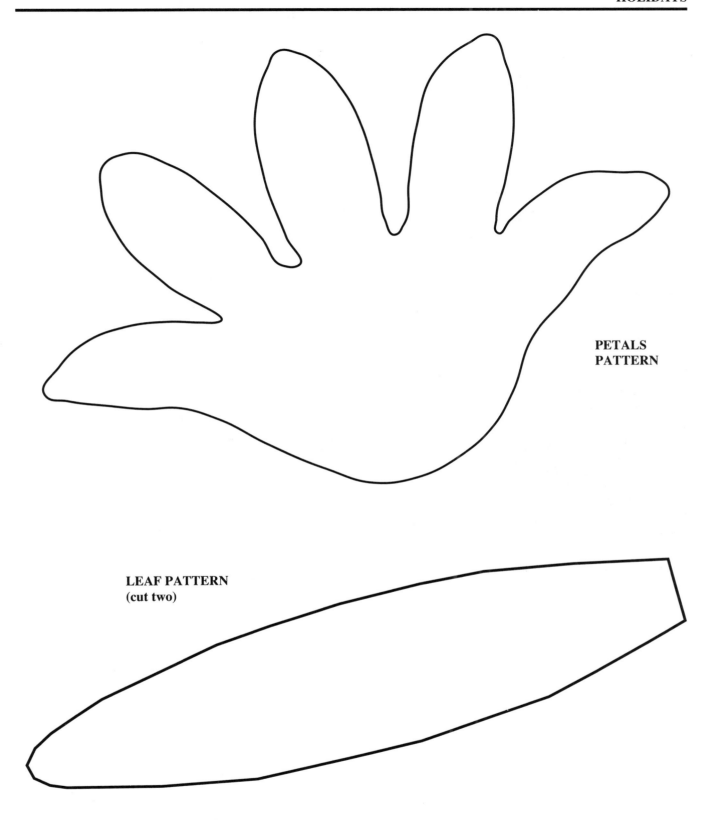

**PETALS
PATTERN**

**LEAF PATTERN
(cut two)**

# SPEAKING FROM THE CROSS

Up on the cross . . . what must it have been like? An inspiring Easter board can be composed of the words Jesus spoke. Share the cross with your church as you celebrate the Easter victory!

Center the cross in the middle of the board. Add a smaller one on each side. Attach a white paper lily to the middle cross and place the message below the crosses. A separate card or piece of paper may be used for each of Jesus' words or group of words. List in appropriate sequence.

**Verse Examples**

1. "Father, forgive them, for they do not know what they do." Luke 23:34
2. "Assuredly, I say to you, today you will be with Me in Paradise." Luke 23:43
3. "Woman, behold your son!" (to Mary) "Behold your mother!" (to disciple) John 19:26, 27
4. "My God, My God, why have You forsaken Me?" Mark 15:34 (quoted in part)
5. "I thirst." John 19:28 (quoted in part)
6. "It is finished." John 19:30 (quoted in part)
7. "Father, 'into Your hands, I commend My spirit.' " Luke 23:46 (quoted in part)

# SPEAKING FROM THE CROSS

examples

# OPEN THE CARD AND OPEN YOUR HEART

At Christmas time, we are called upon to give to others. This board will remind members of the various calls upon our gifts or time. Use Christmas cards, or make cards from holiday-colored construction paper. Size of card will depend upon the number of items featured. Post description of each concern on the inside; label the outside.

**Christmas cards with label**

fold

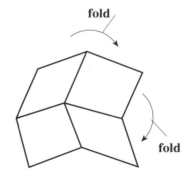

fold

You can make your own Christmas card using the template on page 31. Copy page 31 onto a piece of construction paper. Cut it out and fold where indicated to create your own card.

My Christmas Wish

fold

▼ outside of card

*My Christmas Wish*

fold

fold

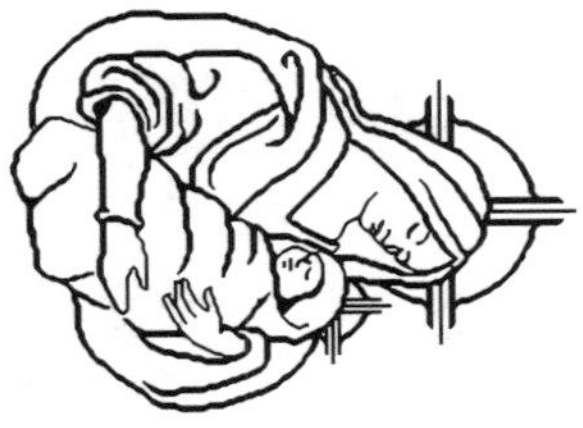

fold

▲ **inside of card**

fold

# MAKE CHRIST THE CENTER OF YOUR LIFE

## MAKE CHRIST THE CENTER OF YOUR LIFE

school pennant     portrait of Christ     notes/reminders

**R**emind members that our lives will have meaning when we make Christ the center of our lives. Find a close-up of Christ in either Sunday school literature or a religious magazine and use it as the center focus. Add some everyday items: dental appointment slip, school pennant, football ticket stub, etc.

# TAKE TIME OUT FOR THE LORD

**T**o stress the importance of religion and worship in our busy lives, remind people that there is always time for the Lord Jesus.

## TAKE TIME OUT FOR THE LORD. HE WILL TAKE TIME OUT FOR YOU.

## HANDS THAT HELPED

examples

# HANDS THAT HELPED

**T**he twelve disciples were very important to Jesus. Emphasize their work in this board message.

On a separate piece of paper, place a picture of each disciple or a picture showing each one with Jesus. Title each sheet with the disciple's name. Place a group picture at the top.

# THE BODY OF OUR LORD

Reveal the human side of our Lord. This board will permit us to see him in body form. Quote Bible version as needed.

**HIS EYES**
What might they have seen?
**HIS FEET**
How weary were they from traveling in Bible lands?
**HIS MOUTH**
Did he thirst?
**HIS EARS**
Did he listen to burdens poured out by the people?
**HIS KNEES**
Were they sore from kneeling?
**HIS LEGS**
Example(s) of standing strong.
**HIS ARMS**
Used to carry our burdens. Extended outward to comfort.
**HIS HANDS**
Offering to others as he shared. His healing touch.

Below the title, list each example, including a picture, a brief description, and Bible verse(s).

Note: A picture of the total Jesus would add emphasis to the message.

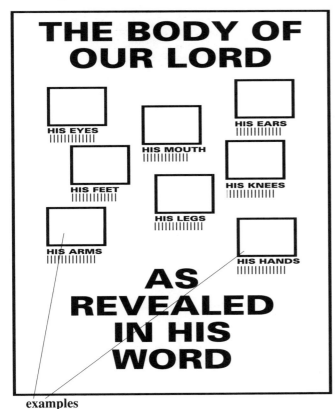

examples

# "THIS IS MY FATHER'S WORLD"

Songs from your church hymnal add perk to any bulletin board, not to mention the fostering of "harmony" between church members!

Board space may limit your choices. Consider these options:

**1. Print the entire song; if lengthy, type.**
**2. First line of song, with picture related to the message.**
**3. First verse of song.**
**4. A popular refrain.**

"And He walks with me,
And He talks with me,
And He tells me
 I am His own;
And the joy we share
As we tarry there,
None other has
 every known."
From:
"IN THE GARDEN"

picture

## DON'T <u>B</u> FLAT

Encourage members to join and/or try out for the choir(s). Post photos of the choir(s) in concert. Include a message listing time and place for audition.

pictures/try-out time/place

DON'T <u>B</u> FLAT

JOIN THE CHOIR

## THERE'S ALWAYS TIME FOR PRAYER

THERE'S ALWAYS TIME FOR PRAYER!

number squares/examples

This would be most eye-appealing if done in the fashion of a clock.

# ALL THE NEWS WE PRINT TO FIT!

**M**ost churches mail a weekly news bulletin to members. Honor the volunteers who assist in this important function. Post photos—at work, if possible—list name and job description. Also list deadlines/details for turning in church news. This can be mentioned separately, centered among the photos. The familiar words of the title suggest the hard effort of the volunteers.

message about deadlines/etc.          photos with name/
                                       job label, etc

# BEGIN TO LIVE WHEN YOU BEGIN TO GIVE

**L**et your members come "alive" after they accept the challenge offered by this board! As the title suggests, only after they "give," will they be able to "live" a more happy and content life.

Below the title, list ways members can serve both inside and outside their church home.

**\*asterisk can be made from small strips, placed in like manner.**

message note lists opportunities

# GROW AHEAD . . . OPEN IT!

**N**o one can turn away from a gift! We open it quickly, eager to see what's inside! How much better life would be if we were to take this same approach elsewhere:

**OPEN THE BIBLE**
**Gain knowledge and understanding.**
**OPEN THE CHURCH**
**Many good things await us inside!**
**OPEN TO GOD**
**Gain a sense of inner peace.**
**OPEN TO OURSELVES**
**We would be refreshed.**
**OPEN TO OTHERS**
**Feel a sense of purpose as we reach out to help those in need.**

These gifts are easy to make! Wrap a rectangular piece of poster board in gift paper and top with a bow!

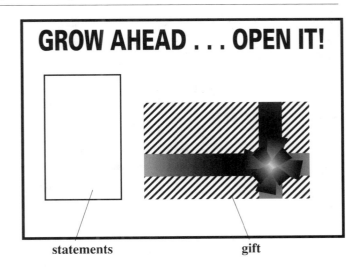

statements                    gift

# WATCH YOUR INTEREST GROW!

**P**romote church attendance! Use green construction paper for the dollar bills. Neatly pen examples of service on the dollars. The rectangular shape illustrates growth. Remind members that just as their money grows when they contribute to savings, so their church interest will grow when they invest in the opportunities offered in the church:

examples of personal church investment

rectangular shape illustrating growth

# REMEMBER TO SHARE

**T**his theme idea is a reminder to give outside of the church. Illustrate with appropriate pamphlets and brochures. Quote sources when using statistics. Offer volunteer opportunities to those interested.

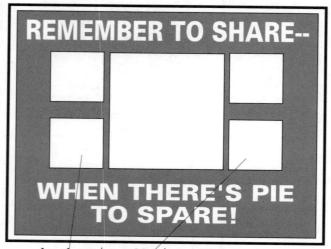

brochures/pamphlets/opportunity notices

# YOU WILT IF YOU WON'T

**T**his board will remind members of the importance of church participation. Illustrate with flowers: Wilted flowers suggest a lack of church participation; a flower in bloom reminds us of the inner change and blossom that comes from church participation.

flower box with wilted flowers

red letters on green paper stems

flowers in bloom

# HOW FAR YOU'LL THROW —HOW FAR WE'LL GROW!

How far will our church dollar take us? How many "ripples" does it have? Will we toss out a little pebble, or a stone of more weight? Use circle rings to represent ripples; fashion stones from bits of paper. Allow room for charts, lists, etc., as desired by your church.

paper "rocks"    blue paper background    "splash"

paper ripples

# A CHURCH IS AS ABLE . . .

Monetary pledges and gifts are vital to any church. Our concerns about stewardship will determine how well our church stands. Likewise, a table stands with support from the legs. Use a table and this catchy title to encourage members to give.

stewardship message

table made of colored paper

# BE OF GOOD TASTE . . .
# PLEDGE!

After viewing this board, members should have a "taste" of the importance of stewardship! Below the title, feature a bowl of soup. Accent with paper spoon, napkin, and placemat. Include the message about stewardship.

placemat

napkin

## BE OF GOOD TASTE . . .
## PLEDGE!

## A SOUPER IDEA!

soup, bowl, spoon, and
vegetables of colored paper

message

# A PENNY FOR YOUR OUGHTS

Promote church stewardship with this board idea. Center a gumball machine as the focus, and place a stewardship message on each side. You might attach a strip of five real gumballs to each side of board.

Use white for border and lettering. Use a coin to cut a pattern for the gumballs, and tape them on a large circle. Cut and bend a square for a flap to lift for "gumballs"; a half-circle for a coin to go in the "slot."

gumballs cut from colored paper

A PENNY FOR YOUR OUGHTS

STEWARDSHIP

paper flap to lift for gum

message

# FOR THE BEST SEAT IN THE HOUSE

A "movie" pass will admit everyone to Sunday school class! Post tickets below the title.

FOR THE BEST SEAT IN THE HOUSE!

tickets (class name/room number on each)

# GET IN SHAPE!

This board is ideal for use at the beginning of a new year, when weight-loss motivation is highest! Use circles, squares, rectangles, and triangles—cut from construction paper—to represent each Sunday school class.

GET IN SHAPE!

various color paper shapes

class name

## IMPROVE YOUR OUTLOOK ON LIFE . . .

This "vision" chart will help fill your Sunday school. You may wish to fashion a pair of "glasses" with the double "o" found in "school."

**Answer: Improve your outlook on life; attend Sunday School.**

M

PRV

YR

OTLK

N

LF

ATTEND

SUNDAY SCHOOL

## BRIGHTEN UP YOUR LIFE!

Promote Sunday school attendance! Blue would be a preferred background color. Use yellow or white for accent. A light bulb or light switch would highlight message.

real or colored paper light bulb with paper strips for accent

BRIGHTEN UP YOUR LIFE!

SWITCH ON TO SUNDAY SCHOOL!

colored paper light switch

## SEE U IN S NDAY SCHOOL

Let members' eyes do a double-take after they read this clever message! The missing "u" in Sunday represents each absent member. Members will take the hint and participate in the class of their choice.

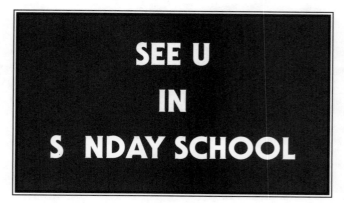

SEE U

IN

S NDAY SCHOOL

# TO GROW . . . GO!

**S**unday school attendance is sure to improve with this clever board idea! The underground roots of a tree will feature the names of classes.

To show dirt below the grass, use a light orange paper. Attach class names (written on strips) neatly to the roots.

tree of green
paper

blue paper background

white paper clouds

class names attached to roots of tree

# ALL TIED UP?

Using two shoes knotted together, remind members that we too sometimes feel the same way! A "knotted" uptight feeling is uncomfortable. We too need to "unlace" . . . and what better place than in Sunday school class!

Cut two shapes by tracing around a shoe placed on the paper. Attach a paper strip (sized in proportion to the shoe) to each. Join in knot fashion with the letter X. Post as if dangling.

Note: Substitute a pair of children's shoes, if you'd like!

# FREE PARKING!

Use strips of paper to simulate a parking lot and title. Paper car could be placed at side, ready to park!

Include a list of class names and room numbers. A visitor would appreciate this.

**"parking lot" of white paper strips**

**cars of different colors**

# IT'S UP TO YOU!

Fashion an elevator door from a rectangular piece of posterboard. Trim edges with paper strips for accent and top with two arrows, pointing in opposite directions. Elevator buttons (thumbtacks), signifying choice, should be to the right of the elevator. Beside the buttons, place a list of classes offered. Members can choose which class to attend!

elevator door    thumbtacks    list of Sunday school classes offered

# TRY SUNDAY SCHOOL— YOU'LL LIKE THE CHANGE

For this board message, make a dollar-bill change machine. A standard-size piece of poster board is ideal. Coins of round pieces of paper will spill from a change box (a square piece of paper). A dollar bill crafted of green construction paper is about to "enter" the bill slot (a strip of paper). On each coin, list a change to occur as a result of class attendance. SUNDAY SCHOOL should be written on the dollar.

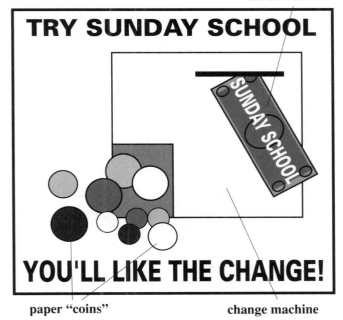

"dollar bill"

paper "coins"      change machine

# UP AND BAT 'EM! TOUCH BASE IN SUNDAY SCHOOL

Promote Sunday school attendance with this board idea. Everyone who obeys this message can become a "winner." Use the ball-field diagram.

description of classes

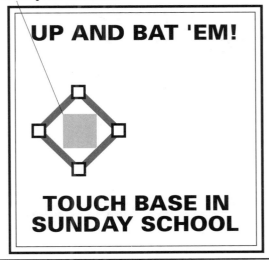

# A STEP FROM THE STEEPLE . . .

Haven't we been told to go forth and spread the word of God? Emphasize the importance of evangelism. Place a pulpit outside the front door of a church. Use light blue for the background paper and add a bush or tree. The outdoor pulpit challenges us to tell others about God; a paper sidewalk offers an open invitation.

This building would nicely complement a medium-sized board. Decorate with steeple, cross, and stained-glass windows. Accent with front door and a touch of greenery!

stained-glass window cut from magazine

church, steeple, and cross made of colored paper

pulpit

# GET THE SCOOP?

Worship and Bible study are often overlooked by people in today's world, caught up as we are in day-to-day routines.

This theme shows how we can improve our lives, if we but taste of Bible passages, prayer, and so on.

On each "scoop" of ice cream, list something that will improve our life:

**Bible study**
**church attendance**
**prayer**
**service to the church**
**being kind to others**
**monetary gifts to the church**

printed examples

ice cream "scoops" of colored paper

colored paper cone

# ADD SOME SLICE TO YOUR LIFE

This board offers helpful guidelines for young people. Use a favorite of youth everywhere—pizza—for the illustration. Each slice will show a way to make their lives "tops":

**friends
hobbies
part-time jobs
church attendance
daily prayer
Bible study
community/church
    service
respect for home
    and family
strong moral beliefs
academic achieve-
    ment**

List an example on each slice. Center pizza in the middle, garnish with toppings, and divide into equal slices. Red would be an eye-catching background color. Use yellow or orange for the pizza, then add the colorful toppings-sausage, bell pepper, etc.! Be creative!

**examples (written on some of the toppings)**

# IT DOES MATTER IF YOU CLIMB THIS LADDER!

Remind the church youths of the important virtues to be practiced in life. This idea would challenge them to reach the top! A quick ladder can be made from construction-paper strips. On each rung, neatly print an example of a positive virtue that we should hold:

> **Love others.**
> **Be responsible.**
> **Serve your church.**
> **Obey your parents.**
> **Take pride in yourself.**
> **Show community pride.**
> **Be honest.**
> **Worship.**
> **Study your Bible.**
> **Pray daily.**

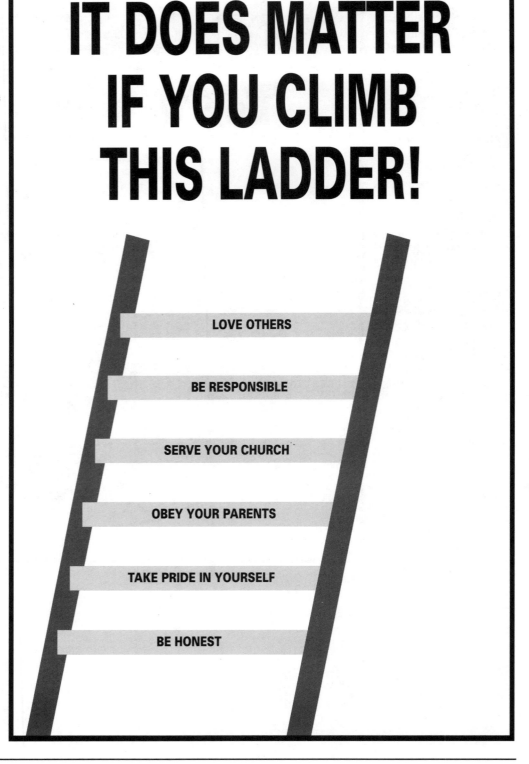

# CHOICE: ACT NOW— PRAY LATER

Today our young people are faced with life-shaping choices—college, career, marriage, to name but a few. This board message is a subtle but strong reminder to plan carefully before making a decision. Use this board when youths are studying the importance of choice. It can be a springboard for many opinions when thrown out for discussion.

# YES—YOUTH!

Promote community-related activities involving youth. This board message underscores the importance of giving, with benefits received by all.

Open the door to the involvement that abounds in the community. Volunteer services demand outside help. Maybe there are options away from the community—a mission group?

A youth meeting, spurred by this idea, can answer and explain. Invite speakers, if possible, and decorate a table or two with appropriate pamphlets and brochures.

*or*

Honor and recognize the talents of the young as displayed by their service(s). Post photos with a brief description tacked neatly below. Use a small map, if necessary, to emphasize work away from home.

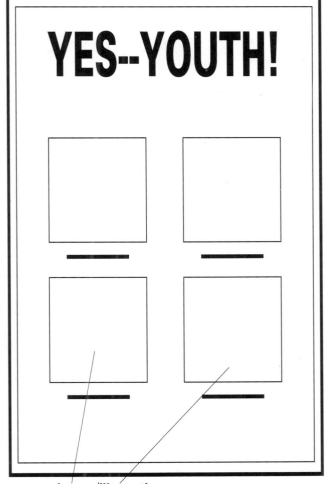

**pictures/illustrations with label description**

# A PERSONAL WORD

With God's instrumental help, this book has become a reality. In prayer, I offer my words of gratitude, as my heart remembers once again that He is always present.

You didn't have to tell me, Lord. I felt our merging partnership when your gentle nudging Spirit handed me paper and pen. "Okay," I declared, "but you'll have to help, too!"

On many occasions, I've seen evidence of your promise, God. I picked up cues, followed your suggestions and relied upon my own experience.

We now have a book. Feeling a twinge of excitement, I put it aside; I must not forget the intent of my writing.

So many things await you. An inner reward of pride will blossom when you begin to beautify your church home.

Become more aware of His love for you. Be prepared for a feeling like no other when you realize that He had to turn to YOU for help!

I never envisioned myself as a writer, but He did. The job was tedious, sometimes filled with distractions. Just barely a year ago, my family and I had our home destroyed by a tornado.

In praise for His presence, we thanked Him profoundly that lives and family photos were spared. But, there was to be more . . . .

Crawling through a bedroom window, I spied the gray box which held the pages of a beginning manuscript. Safe from the storm's fury, I took this as a sign that God approved of my book. A determination never before felt erupted as I left.

**I was on my way!**

**Bonne Morris
December 1989**